Transformation

From a Caterpillar
to a Butterfly

Brenda A. Burton

B & B Publishing

Published by:
B & B Publishing
P. O. Box 1615
Jacksonville, NC 28541

In conjunction with:
Old Mountain Press, Inc.
2542 S. Edgewater Dr.
Fayetteville, NC 28303

www.oldmountainpress.com

ISBN: 978-0-9759420-0-0
Library of Congress Control Number: 2004095272

Transformation: From a Caterpillar to a Butterfly

First Edition
Printed and bound in the United States of America by Morris Publishing •
www.morrispublishing.com • 800-650-7888
1 2 3 4 5 6 7 8 9 10

Dedication

T O MY DEAR BROTHER, John Quincy Burton, I miss you a whole lot. I know that you are up there in heaven decorating. I will never forget riding on my bike with you riding on the handle bars. You told me to let go and you would guide me. I let go and you guided me right into that big pole. I will never forget my dear brother who followed me home one night to make sure I made it there safely. Even though following me home added extra hours to your time, thank you.

To my daddy, Johnny Burton, I cherish the last year we spent together. I know you are in heaven playing your guitar in the heavenly band. I know you are making that guitar sing as you usher in the presence of the Lord. I miss you daddy. The last year we had together made up for all those years we were apart. I miss you calling me, too.

To my daughter, Miranda Ann Burton, I love you and thank you for accepting me as your mother. I know that I wasn't the best mom, but I did the best that I could. I am sorry that I didn't have a college fund saved up for you. I am sorry that your daddy doesn't do right by you. God has been taking care of us in spite of. I thank God for you everyday. I will never forget the day we were riding to church and I looked over at you and you were smiling because you were big enough to ride in the front seat. One day you will be preaching God's

Word; I see it all over you. I am so proud of you. Keep caring for and helping people.

To my mother, Marion Burton, I love you and thank you for giving birth to me. Thank you for running back and forward to the doctor's office with me. I know you did the best you could for me. I thank you for accepting me, even before God delivered me. You showed me nothing but love and I thank you for that.

To my big sister, Joyce Cox, I love you and thank you for having me as your sister. I also thank you for having my back when I was too scared to fight. You have been a big sister. Thank you for coming to the hospital and laying hands on me and casting out those devils in me. You fought the devil for me, and I am so grateful for that. Now, we can fight the devil together.

To my baby sister, Sandra Williams, I love you and thank you for having me as one of your big sisters. We have been through a lot of things together. I am so sorry about tearing up your pictures (Prince). You were a beautiful bride, and I pray that your marriage lasts forever. I know my day is coming too.

To my half sisters and brothers, Linda Burton Thompson, Lil' Johnny, ToJohnnica and Torrance, I love you all and I thank God for you, too.

George Gilmore, thank you for accepting me as your daughter. Love you!

Acknowledgments

TO BISHOP PAUL S. MORTON SR., thank you for being a pastor after God's heart. Thank you for being my spiritual father. Whenever I needed something you were right there. I thank you for teaching me how to stay saved. You taught me how to be a leader and a minister. I am so grateful for your leadership and your love.

To Co-Pastor Elder Debra B. Morton, you have been my spiritual mother. You taught me how to be a woman of God, how to look like a woman of God, and how to carry myself as a woman of God. After all those years of dressing like a man, I had no clue how to dress until I met you.

To Pastor Lester Love, I really thank you for teaching me how to serve a man or woman of God. I watched you while I was at Greater St. Stephen. You served Bishop Morton with a spirit of excellence and you never missed a beat.

To Pastor Leon Senegar, you saw what was in me before I saw it. I thank you for every word that you spoke into my life. I thank you for every prayer that you prayed. I thank you for always being there for me. I appreciate the life that you live for God. I was able to see God use you and I knew that the same God could use me, too.

Pastor Abner Fortson, I really thank God for you. Without your seeds this book would not be possible. Thank you for every encouraging word and your faith in me.

Pop & Dot Silver, you all have been nothing but a big blessing to me. Thank you for putting up with me in Philly.

Stir up the Gift Ministry, Thank you for everything you have done in my family life. I'm glad I took your advice about adding color to my life.

Karl Davis (KinKo's), thank you so much for everything.

Dee, my personal stylish, thank you for always having my hair looking good. Love you.

To all the people that God used to speak into my life, to all the people God used to sow into my life, I love you all. I thank God for using you at that moment to speak into my life. Continue to let God use you. I love you and thank you so much.

To my dear friends that God used to make this book come to pass, without you it would have remained just a vision. Because you saw the vision and planted a seed, your harvest will be multiplied 100-fold God bless you and keep you.

Thanks goes out Gail Brady for her editing services.

Thanks goes out to Tanaka Penn, my niece who re-edited the book on 9/13/04.

Foreword

IF YOU ARE SEEKING DELIVERANCE FOR YOURSELF, a friend or a loved one then, keep turning the pages. In this book Minister Brenda Burton shares her life-changing testimony and victory of overcoming a homosexual lifestyle. Her boldness to take a stand and walk in her deliverance for years has helped those who feared the reality of publicly announcing their deliverance. She has been an example for many men and women who desired to live a lifestyle that is pleasing in the sight of God. I have had the privilege to witness God's transforming power in her life, and to see her become the woman that God intended is a joy. The enemy seeks to bind us permanently but I am confident that after reading this book you will gain a complete understanding of how we can take a struggle and turn it into triumph.

~ Bishop Paul S. Morton, Sr.

The author putting a starter in her 76 Camaro.

Contents

CHAPTER ONE

THE BIRTH

I titled this chapter "The Birth" because a miracle baby girl named Brenda was born to change the world.

O N JUNE 4, 1961, the second baby girl was born to the late Mr. Johnny Burton and Mrs. Marion Burton. *I was anointed and appointed in my mother's womb for the work of the kingdom. See, the devil tried to kill me long ago, because he knew that I would do damage to his kingdom.* I was the second child of four children born to my parents; my oldest sister is Joyce Cox. My baby sister is Sandra Williams. My brother is the late John Q. Burton, who died in a car accident on January 20, 2001. My half sisters and brothers are ToJohnnica and Lil' Johnny, both from New Orleans. Linda Burton Thompson resides in Tampa, Florida. My brother Torance lives in Atlanta, Ga. To the late Ann Burton, who died several years ago. I have other brothers also across the USA.

I was molested by my female cousin (who is deceased now) at a very young age, and I could not talk until the age of seven. When I did speak, I would stutter. I was a sickly child growing up. I stayed at the doctor's office and hospital. I was born with two pelvic kidneys and scoliosis. The doctors told me that I could never have any children because of my pelvic kidneys. My mother took me to a lot of speech therapists to find out why I would not talk. When I did finally start to talk, I stuttered. Words would not come out right. I could say the words right in my mind, but when they came out it sounded like Brrennda. People made fun of me all the time. I was baptized at the age of twelve (12). My mother raised me in church all of my young adult life. I remember riding to church for choir rehearsal every Saturday with my sister, aunts and my step grandmother.

*Names mentioned in this book have been changed for sake of privacy.

I sang in the youth choir and I attended church on Sunday. At Vacation Bible School, they asked the youth to quote Bible verses. I was able to quote St. John *14:1-5* which became my favorite chapter in the Bible. I was able to quote it by heart: *"Let not your heart be troubled: ye believe in God, believe also in me."* I got the opportunity to attend a youth convention out of state. It was really good. I thought that I was the perfect little girl growing up. My memories from my childhood had been blocked; I only remember bits and pieces. As I write this book more memories are being loosed in Jesus' name. *(April 20, 2004 I remembered that I was molested by my female cousin)*

One day my biological daddy stopped by my mother's house. I was so excited to see him, until I found out he was not staying *(my mother had already remarried, but I didn't understand)*. My father was only there to bring my sister and I $500 dollars. I did not want his money, but of course, I needed it. I became angry when I found out that he was not staying. I wanted my daddy's love so badly. I just wanted to be able to call my father "daddy." I had no one else to call daddy. I don't know why, but I would not call my stepfather daddy. I always wanted my biological daddy to be there while I was growing up.

All my friends at school would talk about how their daddy would do this and that for them. I just wanted to be able to say that my daddy was doing things for me. The kids at school would say things like *"My daddy is going to take me to the game, my daddy is going to take me shopping, my daddy loves me so much, my daddy took me to the park."* I just wanted my daddy's love so badly, just to have him talk to me: What I wanted didn't cost a lot of money, just time. Having a step-dad was not the same as having my own daddy.

The s*pirit of rejection* kicked in, and I felt like my daddy didn't want or love me. I do not remember my daddy even coming back to my mother's house after stopping by that day to say he was leaving. My mother gave me love, but I needed my daddy's love. Because my daddy wasn't there, I wanted to become him. I figured if I was a boy, then my daddy might want me.

I used to play with all the boys in the neighborhood. I would climb trees with them, and I was so good that everybody started calling me tomboy. I used to wish that I was a boy, and would pretend that I was one a lot of the time. I can remember trying to use the bathroom like the boys do. I also recall looking at the girls' butts in high school. I did have boyfriends in high school, but I never really fell in love with them. I saw the way my aunts and cousins would be abused and misused by guys and I didn't want to go through that heartbreak. Finally one day, I met this guy name Mark*. He was kind of cute and I fell in love with him before I knew it. He broke my heart, too. I found out that he was dating my cousin and me at the same time. I was so hurt that I said to myself, "Never again will this happen to me."

I played church as a child growing up and I always wanted to be the preacher, but I didn't know why. *I never thought that I would become a preacher, but I did know that I would do something to change the world.* Church was very important in my childhood, until I went off to college, and that is where the story begins.

CHAPTER TWO

THE BEGINNING

I titled this chapter "The Beginning" because it was the beginning for me being on my own, so I had choices to make.

I WILL NEVER FORGET when my mother and great grandmother, Margie, dropped me off at the dormitory. I looked out of the window as they were pulling off and became so sad. Here I was left all alone at this university where I knew no one. I was a young lady in college who had not really experienced life. I was on my own. It was up to me to decide if I was going to class. I had to do it all by myself. I cried for awhile and then began to pull myself together. I met friends on the same floor that day which felt the same way. *I just believe the enemy was setting up his territory, planning his strategies on how to attack me.*

My first year there was okay. I met a lot of people and it went by really fast. I didn't have a television in my room, so I watched the TV in the lobby. One evening while watching TV, I fell asleep. A hand rubbing between my legs awakened me. I tried to scream, but nothing came out. I told this man to stop touching me, but he would not. He said to me, *"You know you enjoy me touching you. I can make you feel real good. Just take me up to your room."* I pushed his hand off of my legs. He told me not to tell anyone. He said to me, *"If you say that I touched you, then I will get you later. No one would believe you anyway.*" I just stared at him. I asked him, "What else did you do to me?" He just laughed at me and said, "*You better not tell.*" I didn't even know his name. I had no idea who and why this man would even touch me. I was scared and I never told anyone until now.

One Friday I started to miss my family, so I drove home for the weekend. I went out to a club with my cousin, my aunt, and my aunt's friend Jean* (names mentioned in this book have been changed for the sake of privacy). As we were sitting watching other people dance, my aunt and cousin got up to dance.

Jean and I were still sitting at the table. Suddenly I felt a hand rub across my legs. I wanted to scream, but I froze, I was too scared to say anything. I thought to myself no one would believe me anyway. Jean is so popular with my family. They love her so much, and they will never believe me. I looked at Jean and she just acted as if she wasn't doing anything. I didn't want to start anything between my aunt and her friend, so I said nothing. She continued to rub her hand across my leg. I became so nervous that I just stood up and left the table. As I was walking to the door of the club, I started to think, "Why would my aunt's friend touch me on my leg?" I was really scared about going back to the table. I was asked to dance and that took my mind off things. I was having a good time and I had forgotten about Jean. I glanced over at the table to see what Jean was doing and she was staring right at me. I stayed on the floor until I got tired of dancing.

When I finally went back to the table, I changed my seat. Jean got up and went to the bathroom. She came back and sat next to me again putting her hand on my leg as before. I became upset this time and I just looked at her as to say,

"Please, take your hand off my leg." I knew that if I had told my aunt and cousin, it would have been a big fight because they were violent and were well known for carrying razors and using them. I did not want to be the blame for that, so I just didn't mention it to them. I believe that Jean knew that I wouldn't tell, that's why she kept on touching me. When I would go to the bathroom, she would come to the bathroom as if she had to use it. When we were all sitting at the table my aunt began to say things like, "Jean is my best friend," I thought to myself, if she only knew. That was the first contact, as an adult, in which a woman touched me. I never told anyone this; as a matter of fact, I had forgotten about it until I started to write this book.

The next year I met several boys. I met this guy named Harry*. He was very handsome with big muscles. We went out a couple times, but I stopped seeing him because he wanted me to sleep with him. I was introduced to Alvin* by my friend's, boyfriend. He was such a gentleman. We discussed our feelings toward each other. We decided to date. We dated a long time and everyone knew us as a couple.

Alvin finally told me that he had never slept with a woman before and that he wanted me to be the first. I was glad because I wanted a man to be gentle with me. I told him that I would teach him everything that he needed to know (as if I knew a whole lot myself). He was very kind to me. Whatever I wanted or needed, he was there to provide it for me. We dated for a long time. I even went to meet his parents. Unfortunately, his parents did not approve of me because I was outspoken. They were very high-class people with a lot of money. His mother told me that they were high-class people, and that she wanted Alvin to marry someone that was high-class also. The battle was on from that moment. Every time we would have a disagreement, she would jump in. On the other hand my family really loved Alvin. They thought that he was the best thing that ever happened to me.

Finally, one semester he didn't come back to school. I wrote to him every week, but there was no answer. I knew that his mother might not give him the letters, yet I had no idea what was going on. All I knew was that he was in love with me before he left. Another semester went by. He wasn't back and still there were no letters. His mother had finally won. I began to feel rejected again, I even tried to commit suicide several times in the dormitory and was rushed to the hospital. I tried to end my life more than ten times. I would take an overdose of pills, but I had tried it so many times that eventually I did not even get sleepy. The school told me that I needed to get a letter from a psychiatrist if I wanted to return to school. My family knew the president of the university, and he approved the letter from my mother instead of a letter from a psychiatrist, and I was back in school the next semester. *This is when I think the spirit of suicide came in.* I do not recall anything else happening after that. I went on with my life and continued to go to class.

CHAPTER THREE

THE BEHAVIOR CHANGE

I titled this chapter "The Behavior Change" because my behavior changed toward women and I became a lesbian.

I HAD THIS CLASS THAT I really enjoyed going to, then I had death in my family. My grandfather died, which caused me to miss a lot of days from school. The professor I had was so mean to me. She would give me a lot of extra work. She even had an attitude as if I was bothering her. I had to end up going to her boss. Her boss made her spend extra time with me and she hated it. She made me so mad, I began dreading going to her class. We exchanged numbers so that I could call her to schedule time off campus to try and catch up. I started waiting for her (Maxine*) after class. There were always a lot of students waiting for her. She was a very popular teacher. All the students loved to be around her. She made them laugh, but when it came to me, she was so serious.

I will never forget how I began having feelings for her. I had never acted on those types of feelings before. I always wanted to be a boy growing up, and I was always called a tomboy, at least that is what my family told me. I became ashamed of the way I started to feel. I said to myself, "Hey, you should not feel this way toward a woman." I became so confused that I dropped her class. Later, I received a phone call from Maxine. I was so excited to hear from her. We would talk for hours on the phone. She asked me, "Why did you drop my class? You had a good grade." I told her that I couldn't handle her class (to be honest I couldn't handle the way I was feeling about her). We continued to talk almost everyday. The girls in the dorm were becoming angry with me because I stayed on the phone too long. I was falling in love with her. I would go to my other classes and just daydream about her. I had begun to feel like I was in a dream. I felt like I was here, but I really wasn't able to make contact. It was hard to explain. I was crying for help and no one could hear me. I felt just like I was in a daze or a trance; like I was losing my mind.

I dropped all of my classes that semester, and just remained in my dorm. *This is when the demon took over my mind.* The only time I would leave was when she would call me.

The next semester I was able to go to class, and I registered for Maxine's class again. Of course I passed her class with a good grade. We talked on the phone every day and night. Then one day I found myself waiting on her so that we could go to the motel. We had made plans to be together that night and I couldn't wait. Time was growing closer and I found myself getting afraid. I recall sitting in my car waiting and waiting. Then finally Maxine came out, walking toward my car. My heart started to beat very fast as we drove to the motel. I parked the car in the back and walked around the front of the motel to check in. We went into the room and that was the last thing I remember. This *is when the demons entered into my body.* I woke up the next morning and I didn't remember anything. It was as if I had blacked out.

She had to tell me everything that happened that night. After that night, I was in love with her, and no one could keep us apart. Everywhere she went, I went. Everywhere I went, she went. We became an *item*. I hardly went to class because I constantly thought about Maxine. I was suspended from school because of my grades. I refused to tell my mother that I was not in school, because I knew that she would make me come home and I couldn't leave Maxine for a whole semester. So I stayed at the college, but not in the dorm. I had nowhere to live, (I was homeless) so I slept in my car for a few days. Then Maxine let me in her window to sleep for a night. Her parents would not allow me to stay overnight because of all of the rumors about their daughter and me. The next night, I dared not try to sleep overnight. I was afraid we might get caught. I asked an old male friend whom I knew liked me if I could stay overnight with him. He said yes. I was so afraid he would make me have sex with him, and after getting through that night safely, I refused to stay there another night.

The very next night I went to live with another male friend. He was so happy to let me stay the night there. He also had two roommates that were males. I remembered thinking that night so clearly, that if I longed to sleep in a bed and not my car, I knew I would have to give in to him so I prepared myself. (Maxine knew where I would be every second of the day. Each day we spent the entire day together until nightfall). *Now back to my friend's house.* I was so tired. I just wanted to lie down, and as soon as I laid down, he got into bed. We were there for about an hour, then I felt his hand moving on my body. I wanted to scream, "*Leave me alone and don't touch me,*" but I knew if I did, he would tell me to leave his house and I didn't want to spend another cold night in my car, so I allowed him to touch and rub his hands over my body. I really hated every minute of it. Finally he ended up on top of me, and I really don't have to tell you what happened next. I hated it and I felt very bad. I felt like I had cheated on Maxine, but I knew all along if I had refused, I would have to spend the night in my car *(maybe I should have slept in my car, but it was cold and I wanted to lie down in a bed).*

After it was over, I laid in bed thinking what a big mistake I had made. Then I thought about Maxine (*Oh God, what would I tell her?)* Well it was finally morning, and my friend had to go to work. I was so glad I just wanted to go and take a shower and wash his smell off me. After the shower, I called Maxine and pretended that everything was alright. She asked me if he tried to have sex with me, and I told her no. I lied because if I had told her the truth, I would be in trouble. Maxine was a very dominating and violent person. We talked on the phone until I got hungry. I told her that I would call her back after I fixed something to eat. I walked into his kitchen and just as I got ready to fix something to eat, his roommate came in the door. He immediately started flirting with me. The phone rang. It was Maxine I told Maxine that Jimmy was flirting with me. She told me to go in the bedroom and lock the door. She told me to call her as soon as I got in the room. Well, I never made that call. On the way to the room, Jimmy pulled me into his room and locked the door. He threw me on the floor and put his knees on my chest.

He put one of his hands over my mouth, and with the other hand he started taking my clothes off. It seemed as if everything I did made it worst. I begged him, P*lease don't do this, please, "b*ut he kept right on taking my clothes off. I was so afraid. It was as if I was in a horror movie. I couldn't make him stop.

The next thing I remember, I saw a policeman standing over me. Maxine had called the police and they were there in full force. Jimmy was nowhere in sight. The sheets that were on the bed were gone also. I was wrapped up in a blanket and taken to the hospital. They ran all kinds of tests on me. The next stop was the police station. I was too tired to go over the details, so they let me leave until the next day. That night I was able to spend the night with Maxine and her family. *I believe they felt sorry for me.* Then one day, I got a phone call and I was told that if I continued with the charges on Jimmy, all of the information on Maxine and myself would be revealed at the trial. This meant that Maxine would probably lose her job at the university. I had a choice to make; punish my rapist or have my lover lose her job. Maxine told me it was my choice, but she wanted to see that guy punished for hurting me. I made my choice. I couldn't see Maxine lose her good job because of me.

I dropped all charges. I never told my mother about any of this until I called home one day to check on her. She told me that Jimmy's mother had called her and told her. She also told her that I was in college sleeping with this woman and saying that her son raped me. Of course, I had nothing to say. That was the longest twenty minutes I had ever spent on the phone with my mother. Later on, I finally told her the truth, she told me to come home, but I couldn't leave Maxine. I could not stand being away from her for five minutes.

As the days passed, I tried to forget the whole incident with Jimmy, but rumors started flying around. Jimmy and his mother had gone to church and testified about me saying that I accused him of raping me. I was marked as a bad person. Everytime someone would look my way I could hear them talking about me. Then the rumors got even bigger. They said something that did not involve me.

The lie was told that I had been caught with this male professor and he had damaged all of my female organs inside. I was so confused I started to believe the lie. You see *the enemy is so slick that he would have you to believe a lie that you know is not true.* I thought that maybe I could have done it when I wasn't in my right mind. So I went to the professor's job to see if he recognized me. He did not have a clue as to what I was talking about. I felt like a fool as I left that man's office.

CHAPTER FOUR

THE STRUGGLE

I titled this chapter "The Struggle" because of my struggle to stay near Maxine, even if I was homeless.

MAXINE MADE ARRANGEMENTS for me to stay at a hotel. After staying at the hotel for months, they offered me a job there. It worked out perfectly. Every dime I made, I gave it back to the hotel. I had my own private room there. Maxine and I were together every night. She would pick me up after work at the hotel, and we would spend the entire day together. Well, the bills started coming in from my stay at the hotel. Maxine and I had to come up with a new plan. She found some people for me to stay with. I stayed with them for awhile, then one day I saw my friend Harry. He was able to tell that I had changed from two semesters ago. He asked me what was wrong. I began to share with him all I had been through, except about Maxine. He asked me if I would like to stay with him, and in exchange I could get him a job working with me at the hotel. I talked to Maxine about it, and she stated that it would be okay if we had separate rooms. We agreed and we became roommates. I told Harry about me being in love, but I never told him about Maxine. He just assumed it was a male and I never told him any differently.

It was finally Maxine's graduation. She was getting a higher degree so that she could make more money. That night she had planned a big celebration at a nightclub. We decided since her entire family would be there, it would be nice if they saw me with someone else (they were beginning to wonder about us spending so much time together). *We wanted to make them think that I was involved with someone else.* Harry and I went to the celebration together. Harry had no clue what Maxine and I were doing. All along we pretended like we were sisters. Maxine became jealous when Harry and I started to dance, but we kept right on dancing. Then Harry asked me, "Where is your boyfriend?" I quickly responded, "I'm sure he's coming; he is just running a little late."

While sitting in the club, drinking a soft drink, I was challenged to drink a beer. I wasn't a drinker at all, but I got very drunk by just drinking beer. The night was passing quickly and Harry left the club, I stayed with Maxine and I got as drunk as a skunk (if you've ever heard that expression). Maxine finally dropped me off at the trailer. To make a long story short, I ended up in bed with Harry. Here we go again. He didn't rape me; I had sex with him freely. *Look at what alcohol did to me.* The next morning, bright and early, Maxine showed up at the door. I could not find my underwear, and that is what gave me away. My underwear was in Harry's room and she saw them there. I lied so good that I convinced her and she believed me. *Being in that lifestyle you have to continue to lie to cover your sin.*

Months had gone by and school was out. Harry had already gone home for Christmas, and I was planning on leaving the next weekend as soon as my money came. We had a snowstorm and I was trapped in the storm for two weeks. I had no clue how Maxine and I would survive being apart from one another. The phone lines were down and I did not think I would live without seeing or being with her. I had neither money nor food. Then one day, I found ten dollars in food stamps. Boy I was happy! Now I could finally get some food. I walked very slowly to the store because the snow was deep. I had never walked in snow before so I was a little nervous. After falling down before finally making it to the store, I got some meat, cheese, cookies, candy, chips and ice cream. Then I thought, "I only have ten dollars, and this had to last for at least a week." I put back everything except the meat, cheese and bread. I made it back to the trailer and hurried up and fixed a sandwich because I hadn't eaten in two days. I wanted to eat at least three sandwiches right then, but I realized I had a lot of days left before the storm would be over. The storm lasted longer than I thought it would. I ran out of food again and had no money left. I just started to read a Bible that I found, I'm not sure if it was mine or not, but I was just led to read it. All I had to eat was the Word of God. I drank water and read the Bible all day. When the sun went down, I went to sleep. I do not recall having a television in the trailer.

One day I heard the door opened, I knew that Harry was the only one with the other key, and he was still in Detroit. In walked Mr. G*, the landlord. He said he was there to check the pipes so they would not freeze. When he noticed I was living there alone, immediately he pushed me to the floor and started touching my body. He started kissing my body with his nasty lips, I was so afraid. I started to push him off me. He pushed me back on the floor. We tossed and rolled for a while. I pleaded with him not to do that and finally he stopped. He said he would be back to finish the job. I sat there in a corner of the trailer scared to death for hours, wondering if and when he would come back. I finally got up and went to a neighbor's house and told them everything. The neighbor was an African. He really didn't understand everything I was saying, but he stayed at the trailer for a while until we realized that Mr. G wasn't coming back. *I used to think that I contributed to all of these men abusing me. Those red hot shorts I use to wear, they were very, very short, I believe they were called daisy dukes in that day and time. I have come to realize that those men had the problem and not me.*

I was wondering if he would come back. He finally showed up one day, but I wasn't afraid anymore because I was steadily reading my bible and drinking my water. I had gained strength from somewhere, *(I didn't realize that the Word of God had given me strength)*. I was ready for him. He walked in the trailer and he didn't even knock on the door. I told him that I would appreciate it if he would knock on the door before coming in. He looked at me with a strange look *(I guessed the glory of the Lord was showing on me)*. I told him if he touched me again I would tell his wife. He slammed the door and left. I was so proud of myself for standing up to him.

The snow had begun to melt and cars were able to travel again. When I saw Maxine I ran and kissed her. I was so glad to see her. It was as if we had been apart for years, but I hesitated to tell her about my past two weeks. Harry had just come back and I decided to tell both of them about Mr. G. They were mad and wanted to go to his house and tell his wife.

I begged them not to go because I didn't want to go through all of that again. My stomach had a knot in it and had been hurting for months. I wasn't worried about it because I thought it was due to not eating a good meal in about a month. Harry took me to the doctor and I found out that I was pregnant. I told myself this couldn't be true because I was told that I could not get pregnant because of my pelvic kidneys. I was indeed pregnant. *Wow, what would I do? Who would I tell?* I was in shock and I didn't tell Harry until we got back to the trailer. He just looked at me and said, "*I love you and I want to be with you.*" He got on one knee and proposed to me. I just looked at him, thinking to myself, "W*hat would I tell Maxine.*"

School was starting in two more days and I would be able to register. I hadn't been in school since the spring semester and guess who I ran into? It was Alvin. He kissed me on my jaw. I didn't say a word for a while because I was still in shock. I had many questions for him and I really did not know where to start. He started telling me that he had a family emergency which was why he didn't come back to school. He said that when I didn't write him back, he thought that I did not want to be with him anymore, that I did not love him anymore. I couldn't answer him because I was confused and still in shock. He asked me where I was living so I took him to the trailer. When he saw Harry he just stood there with his mouth wide open. I introduced him to Harry and they shook hands. Harry looked at me and said that he was going to leave for awhile so Alvin and I could talk, but I told him not to leave because I did not want to stay there. Maxine decided to drop by. I knew that I could not deal with her at that time. I was already confused and I didn't need to add fuel to the fire. I explained to Alvin everything about Harry, the rape, the attempted rape, my pregnancy, and everything except about Maxine. I just could not bring myself to tell him about her. Within one minute, he proposed to me. I was in tears because I finally had what I wanted so badly, a man to love me for me. I didn't give him an answer because I didn't know what to say at the time, *(but deep down in my heart, I wanted to be with him)*.

I knew the hour was getting late and I had to get back to the trailer before Maxine came by. I did not have a clue as to what I would tell Maxine. I made up my mind to tell her everything I would tell her about the pregnancy, Alvin, and Harry. I just knew that would be the most horrible night of all. Well, she picked me up and we rode around as usual. Then I told her that I had something important to tell her. We went to a quiet spot. She turned the car off, and I just sat there for a while. Then I started telling her everything. She began hitting me until I just fell to the floor of her car. There was silence for a long time. When I touched her face with my hands, I could feel the tears as they streamed down her cheeks. She kept asking me, "Why? Why?" I couldn't say a word. I was so confused and tears were streaming down my face. After crying together for about an hour, she asked me, "*What are you going to do?" You have two men that want to marry you and a woman who loves you very much, so what are you going to do?"* I told her that I loved her very much and I wanted to be with her, but now we had a baby to think about. Maxine told me that she would be there for me, and we could raise the baby together. We also discussed the responsibility of the baby's father (Harry). Later on that night I had wondered if I made the right decision. I was in love with her, but I felt something for Alvin also. I felt like I was between a rock and a hard place.

Because of my pelvic kidneys, I was a high-risk case. I had to go to the doctor every two weeks. Maxine and I decided to let Harry and Alvin take me to the doctor so they took turns driving me. It was a very long 35 miles. Harry and Alvin would come to my dorm and discuss what they were going to do with me. The whole school knew that I had two guys in love with me. Harry became upset with me because he wanted me to be with him only. He started saying I wasn't pregnant by him. The school didn't know about Maxine, they just saw us together everyday and all day. That semester ended and I went back to my hometown to have my baby. I didn't even tell Harry when I went into labor because he wasn't claiming her anyway. The following summer I had my baby girl. I named her Miranda. She was a big baby that looked just like her daddy.

Her lips were identical to his lips. She had a big chest and wide shoulders just like her daddy. I took one look at her and I saw him. Maxine came to visit me and I was so happy. I told everybody about my baby girl being born, except for Harry. He made me so mad not claiming our child.

My mother told me that she would keep my daughter while I went back to college, I told my mother that my daughter was my responsibility and I would raise her myself. I thanked her for asking, but, I knew that I needed to keep her. The next semester my daughter and I attended classes together. Everyone thought she was so pretty, I could not believe that her father would not claim his only daughter. After a while he began to complain that I wasn't letting him spend any time with her, so I started taking her to him in order to get a chance to study with my study group. I would also take her to my mother's house when I had to take finals. I knew my daughter was my responsibility. I had to do whatever it took to take care of her because her father was not helping financially, emotionally or in any way. His family wasn't there for her either, so I found a real nice daycare for Miranda, I had to pay $140 a month for childcare. I would take out student loans that would be enough to cover my educational and childcare expense. I had classes that extended all day and with no one else to watch her, the daycare van would pick her up at 6:00 am and return her home by 6:00 pm.

Years had passed and everything was still the same. Harry and Alvin were still discussing my life as if I had no say. They were trying to figure out which one of them would be with me, while Maxine, my baby, and I were still being together. One semester I wasn't doing well with my grades and I needed to have time to study, so I took my daughter to my mother's house. My mother enjoyed having my daughter at her house. Everyone just loved my baby. Then one day I received a phone call. It was my mother and she was very upset. She told me to sit down. Then she told me the worst news that I had ever heard. My brother-in-law had molested my daughter

I jumped up and hate just filled my mind and body. I was ready to go and kill my brother-in-law. I immediately called Maxine and she was ready to go and hurt him also. I knew then that I hated men. I would never allow another man to touch my body.

When I told Harry, he became so angry. I had to physically hold him down and keep him from going to my hometown. I had never seen him act like that before. I reasoned with him, *"If we go to jail for killing my brother-in-law, who would be there for Miranda while we were locked up? We have to be there for her so that this won't happen again."* He finally calmed down and left the apartment for a while. I didn't see him until early the next morning. He made the comment that if we had stayed together, we might have had another night of making another baby. I went to my hometown to file charges against my brother-in-law and to pickup my child. We finally made it through that trauma, and I was even more protective of my child. I did not want Miranda to go through what I had gone through. I kept her away from strangers. I didn't allow her to be around any men at all.

One day I received a phone call from Harry's parents. They apologized for not being there for Miranda. They asked if she could come and stay with them for the summer. I had to think long and hard about that, especially since we really didn't know them. Miranda wanted to go and stay with them. After much thought, I decided to let her go with them. They came down and we spent two days of extensive time together to become more acquainted. Miranda fell in love with her grandparents, and looked forward to seeing them every summer. They still did not help financially, but they were there for her emotionally. I was so grateful that at least she had an opportunity to spend time with them. I do not remember being with my paternal grandparents. *(Thank God that she didn't have to go through what I went through).*

I began to get more serious about my schooling. I changed my major from early childhood education to social work. I stopped spending so much time with Maxine. We broke up because she was becoming possessive of me, and I couldn't do anything without her becoming jealous. I began to do very well in school. I was preparing for graduation the spring of 1989. I made the honor roll the last semester there. Well, I finally made it. I got my degree. WOW! Not only did it take me 8 years to get that degree, but also my whole life would never be the same. *I found out that I had a learning disability but no one caught it until I started working with children who also had a learning disability.* I had gone from being suspended to probation because of my grades, but I made it.

I entered college as a young, naive girl, but I left as a woman who had been raped, abused, misused, and coming out of the closet (gay) with a child who had been molested. *My college days were the worst days of my life.*

CHAPTER FIVE

COMING OUT

I titled this chapter "Coming Out" because I came out of the closet and started dressing like a man.

I WENT TO NEW ORLEANS for two weeks for a vacation. I just really needed to get away from Maxine. She kept coming around my house. She wanted us to get back together. Once I got to New Orleans, I stayed with my cousin who lived around the corner from a gay club. I really enjoyed the club, and I found myself there every night looking for someone to love.

While I was in New Orleans, I found a job working at a group home. I decided to move to New Orleans. Miranda was staying with my mother until I found a place to live. I started my job and was promoted to supervisor immediately. I forgot about my apartment there at the college. I scheduled two trips to retrieve my items. I was to schedule another trip but I was too busy working and partying and ended up losing all of my important papers and furniture

One night at the club I was told to dress like a man or a woman because a lady told me that she liked me but I looked just like her. *In the gay lifestyle, women who played the female role were called "fish" and women who played the male role were called "butch". Fish dressed like a woman and butch dressed like a man.* I told her that I always wanted to be a boy, so I started to buy all men's clothes. *"I was butch."* Once I walked into the club with men clothes on, the women were all trying to get my attention. I enjoyed all that attention. I looked just like a man and I looked pretty good, too. People were mistaking me for a man and I just loved it! When I would go into a grocery store, I could hear women talking about me. They would say things like: "H*e is handsome, but what if he is a woman."* I would just laugh. One day a couple of young ladies were walking down a hallway of a hotel. I could hear them talking about which one would approach me.

I just kept on walking, then finally, I turn around. Wow! You should have seen their faces. They really thought I was a man.

I finally found a place to live. It was a two-bedroom brick house. I was so excited about my little place. One day, I met a young lady at the gay club. She liked me and wanted to come home with me, but I refused. I really didn't know her, and it was too soon to sleep with her. She continued to come on to me at the club. She even asked a friend of mine if I was afraid of her because I hadn't kissed her yet. I finally began to fall for her. She was a pretty chocolate black girl named Wendy*. I finally brought her home with me. We made love and it was wonderful. I decided to go and pick up my daughter and bring her to live with me. I moved Wendy in as well. She gathered her things from the projects where she lived, and my home was her home. She was very loving to my daughter and me. She cooked and cleaned. My bath water was always ready at the end of the day. Everything I needed was there - I thought.

One day after being together for almost three years, Wendy changed on me. She became very jealous and accused me of cheating. When in fact, I wasn't. I only started cheating on her after she accused me. I hated to come home to hear her nagging. She would argue about anything. It just made me sick. She began to get physical and started to hit me. I refused to hit her back, I did not want to fight. One day when I walked in the apartment, BANG! She hit me in the head with an ashtray! I was bleeding everywhere and she wouldn't take me to the doctor. I walked out of the apartment with my daughter trying to find a way to the hospital. My neighbor was willing to take me and while getting into her car, Wendy leaned over the balcony and yelled, *"If you get in her car, I will bust her window right now!"* My neighbor was not afraid. She told me to get in her car and she would take me to the hospital, but Wendy kept yelling, *"If you get in her car, I will, I will do it."* I didn't want to put my neighbor in the middle, so I drove myself to the hospital. When I got there, my aunt and cousin were there and they were cursing and ready to fight. I told my family that I was okay to keep down confusion.

At this point, I had no idea where my daughter was. I found out later that she was with Wendy. I received 5 to 7 stitches in my head, then I was released to go home. I thought to myself, *"W*here would home be?*"* I finally decided to go back home with Wendy. She threatened that if I ever left her, she would ruin my life. I wanted to leave, but she knew too much about me, so I stayed in that relationship (If *you called it a relationship).*

I would work long hours just to get away from Wendy, but I missed my daughter. One day I went to work and saw the most beautiful young woman named Betty*. I thought I was dreaming. She was so beautiful. I fell in love with her immediately. I just had to have her. It did not matter what I had to do to get her. My plan was to befriend her and win her heart. After much planning, I began to take her out to eat and shopping. We started spending a lot of time together. Betty lived in the back of the group home where I worked. Every day I would get off work and go directly to her house. One day I was sitting on her bed, and I reached to touch her face, but her hand stopped me. She said that she was not gay nor did she want to be, I told her I knew that she wasn't, but I wanted her so badly. I told her that I loved her and that I had to have her. I begged her and she almost gave in. She then asked me this question, *"If I come over to your world (sinful life), would you then come over to my world (Christian life) once we are finished?"* I immediately said "Yes!" (I lied) I just wanted her so badly. I would have said yes to anything. *See, how God worked it out. She did come over to my world, but I also came over to her world and I am so happy that I did.*

I spent all my free time with Betty. Wendy became suspicious about me spending so much time at work. She would call my job all day and night. One night when I got back to the apartment, Wendy demanded that we talk. I was so tired after working so many hours on the job and making love with Betty, that when I got home I couldn't do anything but fall asleep. One night, in particular, she wanted to talk. I was so tired I just turned over and went to sleep. The next thing I heard were knives hitting together.

I jumped up in the bed and Wendy said that we would talk or she would kill me. I told her to put those knives up, then we would talk. After she put the knives back in the kitchen, we began to start our conversation. I told Wendy that I was in love with someone else. She became so angry I had to calm her down. I told her that she drove me to the other woman with all of her accusations. I told her it was over and I couldn't take anymore from her. She began trying to seduce me. I told her no, but she kept on kissing me until I felt myself kissing her back. We made love that night and I was so sorry I betrayed Betty.

I went to work the next day only to find out later that Wendy had called the job about fifty times. She talked to Betty on the phone and asked her if she was the woman I was dating. Betty told her that she was the woman that I had fallen in love with. They talked for a long time. Wendy also told Betty that we had made love. *Wendy had begun to destroy my life just like she said.* My job became frustrated with her calling and Betty was furious with me. I was in big trouble and I didn't know what to do. My job had scheduled a meeting with Betty and me. They had a surprise guest that was coming also, and little did we know the surprise guest was Wendy! She came to the meeting and told one lie after another. My job asked her to stop calling, and she said as long as I worked there, she would continue to call and harass me, so my job had no choice but to let me go. I went back to the apartment and told Wendy that she had to go. I found out later that she continued to call my former job until they let Betty go also.

I met with Betty and made up with her. I told her that she could come and live with me. The day Wendy was there with her U-haul to move her stuff out of the apartment, Betty was there with a U-haul moving her stuff into the apartment. Wendy was furious when she saw Betty. She took my furniture that I paid for and then dragged the Christmas tree down the stairs. I wanted to argue with her but I was so glad to be rid of her. I told her to keep it. I would get better furniture than that. When Betty moved her things into the apartment, we had more than we needed.

That night was peaceful, but we knew we had to go job hunting the next day. I told Betty that I was very sorry for all that had transpired because of me. I told her that I would take care of her, if I had to work three or four jobs.

CHAPTER SIX

THE CHALLENGE

I titled this chapter "The Challenge" because I challenged God that if He could take the desires away, I would serve Him.

I FOUND ONE JOB WHERE I worked third shift, then another working on weekends. Betty bought me a video camera, and I started my own video taping business. I had four incomes coming in. We had so much money that whatever Betty and my daughter wanted, they had. We moved out of that apartment because it had too many memories and moved right across the complex to a townhouse. Life for us was going pretty good. Betty brought me a full size pool table for my birthday. One year we had everything that we needed. There was no lack in our life. *(At least we thought so)* All of our needs were met. We were having extra money to do whatever we wanted, and things were going so well.

Betty and I talked about getting married. We also talked about me having a sex change so people would accept us as a couple. I was willing to do anything for Betty. I loved her so much I would have given my life. Betty was a backslider from the Lord and every now and then she would cry at night. We would have discussions about the Lord not letting her go. She told me that she was praying for me and she wanted me to get saved. We both could be serving the Lord, then maybe she would fall out of love with me. I thought the idea was insane then, *but now we are both serving the Lord.*

She would always listen to this white preacher at night. *I love to listen to him now,* but then, I hated to hear his voice because after she listened to him she wouldn't want me to touch her. Sometime I would tell her to change the station to a black man who was a preacher. If we had to look at a Christian show then I wanted to hear someone black. *I found out later that the man was Bishop Paul S. Morton.*

I didn't understand, but I would tell her that I wouldn't let her go either. I told her that I would die first before I lost her. We would have discussions several times. I would make love to her and she would forget about everything for awhile, then finally she told me the time had come for us to make a decision about her moving out because the Lord was not going to let her go. We agreed to go our separate ways, however, when the date would come for her to leave we would change our minds. The thought of Betty leaving me and having to raise my daughter alone caused me to seek professional help for depression.

Finally, one day, she said *"It's time for me to move out."* I said okay even though I really didn't want her to leave. I had no idea how I would make it without her. I loved her so much that I would give my life. The day finally came when Betty was moving her clothes out. She told me that I could keep her furniture, but she had to go now while she had the courage to walk away. I told her that if she walked out of the door, I would kill myself. She told me, "I love you, but I have to go because God won't let me go." I told her that I don't even know how to cook or take care of my daughter, "W*hat will I do?"* She said to me as she walked out the door, "*I love you*

Brenda but I have to go." I got my gun, turned the safety off, and put it to my head ready to pull the trigger. Then I heard a loud voice say, "*I will never leave you nor forsake you.*" I looked around to see who was talking, then I thought about what my mother told me about God! I put the gun down and cried myself to sleep. After that I went into a deep depression.

After waking up the next morning, I scrambled to fix my daughter something to eat. I had no idea what to cook or how to cook it, so we went to eat out. After spending so much money on eating out, I decided to try and cook something. It was very plain and simple and I know that my daughter didn't like it but she ate it anyway. After speaking with my therapist and discussing me putting the gun to my head, she recommended that I check myself into a hospital. If not, she would have to check me into a hospital, and my stay would be longer.

So I checked myself into a hospital for 7 days where it costs me 1,000 dollars a day. (Betty came back to the house to keep Miranda). The hospital was a private institution where lawyers and doctors would come for help. While in the hospital, Shelia the therapist told me that it was okay to love a woman. She gave me the phone number to a gay church. "*I dialed a lot of numbers before, but I thank God that l didn't dial that number.*" She also told me to remember this: "*That which does not destroy you will strengthen you.*" I became an outpatient for 3 months from 9-5 every day. I was afraid to live in the outside world.

I started listening to the radio and Bishop Paul Morton's broadcast was talking against the gay lifestyle. I was late every morning because I was drawn to listen to his radio broadcast. My deliverance came in steps. While in the hospital, my sister, who is an evangelist, prophesied that I would live and not die and declare the work of the Lord. At that point, I had no clue as to how I would raise my daughter.

One weekend after getting out of the hospital, another patient and I were lying across my bed looking at some books. We were looking for some answers to life's hardest questions. I told my friend that I wanted to see what the bible said about homosexuals. I had a bible dictionary *I don't know where it came from but I had it.* We began to look up different words. When I saw what the bible said about homosexuality, I was blown away. It revealed that homosexuality was wrong in God's eyesight. I just couldn't believe it. All this time, I thought that it was okay. Before I read these scriptures, I did not see my lifestyle as a sin. Since I didn't steal, hadn't killed anyone, loved everybody and treated everybody right, I never thought being in love with a woman would displease God. I began to look up scriptures relating to homosexuality, that was when I found out about Romans 1, Leviticus 18:22 & Leviticus 20:13. I couldn't believe that homosexuality was wrong. I was only in love with women and didn't do anything else. I thought, "How could this be wrong when it felt so right?" I began to pray to the Lord. *I made a deal with God. I told him* **"If you can change me and take away my desires for women, I will serve you"** Little did I know, that God was waiting on an "if" from me.

CHAPTER SEVEN

A NEW BEGINNING

I titled this chapter "A New Beginning" because of my new life with Christ. I am saved and thanking God every moment.

ON SEPTEMBER 5, 1993, I confessed the Lord Jesus Christ as my Lord and Savior. This was the beginning of my new life with the Lord. My neighbor Jenny* asked me one day to come to her house for a women's bible study. I told her I didn't want to because I would feel awkward being the only black person there. I did not want to be the only black female at her house. Jennie came over to my house. She wanted to talk to me. She asked me again to come for bible study. She told me that it would help me out a lot. I decided to go. I didn't say a word. I just listened to what they said. I cried a while, then I left. The next time I went, I had a good time. I didn't cry as much.

The weekend came. My sister Joyce (the evangelist) and Betty came to take me to church. We went to Bishop Paul Morton's church. Because it was late when we arrived, we had to sit in the balcony. When they did the altar call, my sister looked at me and asked if I wanted to walk down the aisles. I wanted to (my heart was beating so fast), but I was so scared. After service, we went out to eat. Joyce and Betty left to go home, but not before I promised them that I would go back to church the next Sunday. The next Sunday, Miranda and I went to church. We were late again and had to sit in the very back. I told Miranda that I would find out what time they started and we would be on time.

I told my family that I would join the church and I wanted them to be there. In November of 1993, I decided to walk down the aisles. My mother, sister, cousin, and aunts were all there. I was so happy that they were there for me. As I walked down the aisle, my heart was beating so fast. It was a long walk for me, but I am so glad I did it. My daughter joined that day also. We were now official members of Greater St. Stephen Full Gospel Baptist church.

We were assigned a big sister whose job was to check on us. I later had a talk with Bishop Morton about how God had delivered me from homosexuality. I was still dressing in men clothing. Bishop told me he wanted me to tell my testimony at their deliverance service.

On January 18, 1994 Miranda and I went to our first deliverance service. They had a deliverance line for people to be filled with the Holy Ghost. I wanted everything God had to offer me, so I went up to be filled. I noticed that Miranda had gone up also. I got filled but I didn't have the evidence of speaking in tongues. My daughter was speaking in tongues, and I was a little disappointed. I knew that I had surrendered everything to God, but for some reason, the tongues would not come. The lady encouraged me not to be disappointed, but of course,I was very upset. I felt like I had let God down.

Bishop Morton asked me if I would give my testimony. I was glad for the opportunity to stand before all those people and tell my story. *(See, I was ready to tell the whole world how God delivered me).* When Bishop Morton called my name and I looked out in the congregation and saw all those people, I became so nervous he had to call my name twice. I finally stood up, and when I put my hand on the microphone. I began to feel energy come from someplace. I started to tell my testimony and I couldn't stop talking. When I finished people stood up all over the church and clapped their hands. I was very shocked to see that kind of response. I wasn't expecting that, but it was good. Bishop Morton gave me a hug and thanked me for being brave enough to come and share my testimony. Bishop Morton got up and addressed the church people on how they want to be so subtle with demons, but said we have to take authority over those demons. After service people came from everywhere to hug and thank me for sharing my testimony.

Minister Leon Senegar asked me that night to join Free Indeed Ministries. Another minister approached me saying, "*I see you wearing big ear rings and lipstick. You will be dressing and looking like the beautiful woman that you are.*" She also said, "*Your misery will become your ministry.*" I told her, "*I don't receive that.*"

She said, "Y*ou don't have to receive it; it is going to happen anyway.*" The next day I was telling God that I loved Him, and He told me to give away all my men's clothing. I gave them to my brother and my nephews, and they just loved them. I wasn't worried about what I was going to wear, I had two old dresses that Betty had given me in case I needed them. I also had a couple pairs of jeans I wore to church. I wasn't worried about how I looked. I was just ready to praise God.

I also had to take all those gay videos that I had recorded at the gay club (I was the video person at the gay club) and throw them into the trash. I just started grabbing garbage bags to put all those gay videos into. The very next week, we went to a deliverance service again. I had my hands lifted up to God saying, "I surrender all." Immediately my tongue started moving by itself. I had no control over it. I began to cry because I knew I was completely filled. I stayed up all night thanking God for giving me a new language.

We started attending church regularly and I found out that Greater St. Stephen Full Gospel Baptist Church wasn't like other churches. They started on time. They had five services on Sunday, two bible studies on Wednesday, and a deliverance service on Friday. I was going to church five times a week. I made a deal with God again. I told God that I loved Him and I was so grateful to be alive. I wanted to bless Him with five dollars every time He would allow me to enter into His house. *I knew that five dollars wasn't that much but I was unemployed.* By attending five services a week, my total giving would be twenty-five dollars a week.

God made sure I had five dollars every time I went into His house. That year, I gave over four thousand dollars in tithes & offerings, and I wasn't even working. There was always something going on at church, and I had to keep up with the weekly bulletin in order to remember every function. I would attend Wednesday morning and Wednesday night bible study. *(I was unemployed for almost two years.)*

The Word of God was so good and I was so hungry for it. I couldn't get enough of it. I spent so much time in my Word. I learned about the books of the bible, and the scriptures became life to me. All I wanted to do was read my bible. I was so excited about Jesus saving me that I just wanted to tell the world about His goodness. I started making signs with scriptures on them, and putting them on the bumper of my car. People would stop me and say, "*I wish I had the courage to do that. I look forward to seeing your car. I am encouraged every week by your signs.*"

One day I got too happy. I had signs everywhere on my car. Minister Leon Senegar (who was also over the Free Indeed Ministies) came to talk to me. He told me he knew I loved the Lord and that I meant well, but maybe I could find signs that were made professionally. He talked to me in love, and I was able to receive what he was saying. I looked at my car and it was a hot mess. I refrained from putting so many signs on my car. I found one sign that I liked and put it on my car.

I remember the first time I heard God's voice; I was in the grocery store and God told me to tell this young man that He loved him. I wasn't sure it was God's voice, so I ignored what He was telling me. I saw the young man walking down another aisle, but I still would not say anything to him. There he was, walking out of the store with his bags. God spoke to me one more time and I moved so quickly, I began to tell the clerk to hurry up and check me out because I had to catch the guy. I ran to my car and drove down the block, and there he was getting ready to go inside his house. You should have seen me driving like a crazy person. I caught him just before he went into his house. When I got out of my car, I told him what God told me to tell him and he just smiled. I felt a whole lot better. I promised myself that I would obey God's voice. It is better to obey Him than to chase someone down.

While reading the church bulletin one evening, I began looking at all the people that were listed in the Sick and Shut-in Ministry, and the Lord told me to write to every person on the list. I thought that I was smart. I wrote one letter and I planned to send the same letter to everyone on the list, but God told me to write each person a different letter. I obeyed God's voice again and wrote each person a different letter.

One day after an evening service Deacon Burnett* asked me if I would go with him to pray with the sick and shut in. He told me that the Lord wanted me to go with him. I told him that I didn't know how to pray for people. He said just pray about it and see what God says. *I prayed about it and I knew that my assignment was to go with him to pray for the people.* The first day we went out to pray, he told me that I would need to fast (*go without food until we finish praying*). The very first house we got to, I noticed something on the table. It was one of the letters that I had written. I began to smile. I told God, *"You set this up"* I told Deacon Burnett that I saw my letter on the table, and he introduced me to the family. He told them that God had ordained this. We went on to see the next family. If I remember correctly, he had four families to see each Tuesday. While going with him for over eighteen months, God told me that He had anointed my hands to lay hands on the sick, and for me to join the Helps Ministry.

I began to work with Bishop Morton and the Helps Ministry when he had deliverance services and when he went out to preach. I recall the first person that I laid hands on; they fell out and I was scared. I raised my hands as to say, *"I didn't do anything but touch her."* As I continued to work with the Helps Ministry, I saw many that were healed and delivered through God using me.

I remember volunteering with the Full Gospel Baptist Fellowship. I would stuff envelopes each day and I really enjoyed it. One day I met a young lady who was also volunteering. We became friends. As a matter of fact, she was my first female friend after my deliverance. Her name was Annetta*, and she had two children, an older daughter, and a son who was the same age as my daughter. We became very close. Our families started to spend a lot of time together. I was proud of myself for having a friend that I didn't want to sleep with. I knew then that I was delivered, and people were able to accept me for me.

On Thursday evenings, I would volunteer to go with my sister to the local jail. Joyce would have me give my testimony. The women would come up to me and tell me they wanted to be free. My sister would tell me to lay hands on them, and they would pass out under the anointing. I went to the jail twice a month. It was wonderful to see God move.

CHAPTER EIGHT

THE PROCESS

I titled this chapter "The Process" because God was changing me slowly to make me look like the woman He called me to be.

ONE SPRING EVENING IN 1994, I went to the uptown location to hear the Word of God again. This guy walked over to me and asked me a question about the next service. His name was Tony*. I believed that he liked me and was just trying to make conversation. I answered his question and he asked me if I was coming back to the night service. I told him yes, of course. Well, after the night service Tony came up to me again. We talked awhile after church. He asked me for my telephone number. We started talking on the phone every night, and I started looking forward to seeing Tony after church.

One day Tony told me that our friendship had moved to another level, then he asked me to be his girlfriend. I began to think, "*Wait a minute this guy doesn't even know where I came from.*" Later that night when he called me, I told him that I had something to tell him. When I saw him I told him about how God had delivered me from lesbianism. He said "*Okay, that is your past, what does it have to do with the present? I care about you and your past doesn't have anything to do with you now.*" He asked me again if I would be his girlfriend. I told him yes and hugged his neck. He kissed me and told me that he loved me. Wow! I didn't know what to do. All I knew was I was enjoying what I was feeling. We were together every Sunday after church. My daughter loved him, too, and they got along really well.

Tony and I would go to my house or his aunt's house after Sunday service and wait for the night service. We started spending a lot of time together. He would invite me to eat lunch with him on Fridays. One Friday he gave me some money. He said that he knew that I wasn't working and he wanted to help me out with some of my bills. I wasn't used to that kind of treatment. Each Friday he would buy Miranda things that she liked, and he would bring me something special. One time it was roses, another time it was an outfit, the next time it was money. Every Friday it was something different. One Friday he brought me a pair of earrings. They were big hoops. I could not wear them. They were too big. I wasn't comfortable with wearing the hoops. Tony took the earrings back and bought a tiny pair. I liked the little ones. They were just my size.

The process was beginning; I don't recall wearing any earrings before. Tony was spoiling me rotten and I just loved it. A year had passed by and Tony and I were still dating. One Friday he told me that he had a big surprise for me. He had an engagement ring for me that really threw me because I wasn't ready for that. He was ready and wanted to marry me. I told him that we needed more time to get to know each other. Tony was very upset. He said that we had been dating for over a year and he wanted to marry me. I told him that I believed that God was calling me to preach His word and I needed to be sure. I told him that maybe later we could get married after I heard God clearly so Tony agreed to wait a little while.

I found a job as a case manager, and I was so busy with the job, that Tony and I were not spending a lot of time together. He didn't like that. Between my job and my helping people, things were not going well with us. Tony got mad and said that he had brought me another ring but the day that he was going to give it to me I was too busy to meet with him, so he took the ring back to the store. Finally, I just took time to think about my life. Tony and I set an evening aside for us to talk. He came to my house and we began to discuss our relationship. We both agreed that we were in love with each other. I told him that I knew God had plans for me, and I had to deal with the people who were still bound by homosexuality, *I don't think that he really understood,* but he agreed to have patience with me.

The phone rang immediately after our conversation. It was my job, and my supervisor was on the phone crying. She was at the hospital. Something had just happened to her niece and she wanted me to come to the hospital and pray with them. I told her that I would be there. I looked at Tony and he said, "O*kay, I understand.*" We walked out of my apartment together and drove off in our separate cars. I trailed him on the interstate until we got to the split. I looked over at Tony and motioned for him to pull over. After we pulled over and I got out of my car and walked over to his car, I asked him if he was okay. He said yes, but when I touched his face, I could feel tears running down. He told me that he was okay, to go ahead and be with the family.

I got to the hospital and the police were there, I stayed at the hospital with them until 3:00 a.m. While driving home early that morning, I couldn't think of anyone but Tony. I was praying that everything was alright with us. When I finally talked to Tony he was angry. With our jobs and me helping people, time together was scarce. We were slowly drifting apart. So I suggested to Tony that we take two weeks apart to seriously think about our relationship. Well, after my two weeks apart I was ready for a commitment. Before I called Tony, the Lord revealed something to me. He showed me Tony dating someone else. I said, "No Lord, that's not true." I made that call to find out if what God had said was in fact true. Tony told me that he had met a young lady during our time apart. I was very upset with him, I told him that we had our time apart to think about ourselves, not about someone else. Tony asked me a question, *"Do you want me to leave her? We just started talking. I can leave her if you want me to."* My heart said, yes leave her, but my mouth said, *"If you are mine, you will be back."* I was still in love with him but he never came back *(I guess he wasn't mine after all).* Later on, I got the news that Tony got married and left Greater St. Stephen Full Gospel Baptist Church and joined a sister church *(Bishop Morton had spiritual sons and daughters whom he helped to start other churches out of his church. These are called sister churches).* I continued to do the work of the Lord.

CHAPTER NINE

THE CALL TO PREACH

I titled this chapter "The Call To Preach" because God had a calling on my life, and I finally answered.

ONE DAY, A REPRESENTATIVE of the Women of Excellence Ministry approached me. She asked me if my daughter and I would speak at the Mother and Daughter Lock In. I was in shock! Of course I said yes, I was happy just to have an opportunity to speak about the goodness of God. I had forgotten that Miranda would be leaving for Detroit to be with her grandparents, so I asked my mother would she be willing to speak in the place of my daughter, if they agreed. Everyone agreed and my mother and I were on program.

My subject was on "Truth" I will never forget it. In my prayer time I was seeking God on what to say, God told me, "He wanted me to call the women forward and have a deliverance line." He said that the women needed to be truthful, and if I was to deal with "truth", we might as well be honest. My mother got up and read a letter that I had written about my Pastor and Co-Pastor. She did really well. Now, it was my time and I was struggling with listening to God's voice again or obeying their voice. You see, I had been given fifteen minutes *(I learned that you don't go over time at my church)*, but I knew what God was telling me to do would take longer than fifteen minutes, so I got up trying to obey man rather than God.

When I opened my mouth, there was no anointing. I was stumbling with my words. I stood up there and told them I was sorry, but I had to do what God told me to do. I looked at my Co-Pastor and she told me to go ahead. I told the women that God said they were not being truthful. I told them that God said they could be delivered from fornication.

I closed my eyes for a few seconds, and women just started coming from everywhere. The altar was full from one end to another with women crying out to God. I was standing there with tears in my eyes. There were two lines of women surrounding the altar. My Co-Pastor looked at me and she asked me if God had told me to lay hands on the women. I immediately said, "No!" He didn't tell me to do that. I was so glad because I was just a sister in the Lord. I wasn't a leader yet.

God messed up the whole program! What was supposed to be fifteen minutes turned into one and a half hours. After all the women got their deliverance, we had a long break. People were just coming up to me telling me that I was so anointed, and how God was going to use me in a mighty way. I was just so glad to have obeyed God's voice. I told God that I would not hesitate again when He spoke.

People started asking me to speak at funerals and church events. People continued to tell me that I was called to preach God's word. While in deep prayer, God told me that He had anointed me to preach His Word, and if I didn't do it I would not be able to do anything else. I told God that I wasn't worthy to stand before His people. God told me, ***"That is why***

I have chosen you to preach my Word because you have a heart of compassion and I will use you to draw My people. "
I finally answered the calling. I went to the President of the Ministerial Alliance Preparatory class, and they told me that I had to preach a five minute sermon in front of them. I preached and they were excited about me. One of the Elders told me that they knew that I had a calling on my life. They were just waiting on me to come and talk to them. I was now an official member of the Greater St. Stephen Full Gospel Baptist Church One Year Preparatory Class.

We were assigned nursing homes to visit and to feed the hungry on Saturdays. I loved it. I would bring my daughter's Karaoke with me so that we would have a microphone. I started feeding the hungry every Saturday because I liked it. I explained to my daughter their situation and she told me that she wanted to help, but she would rather work in the kitchen. We fed two hundred people each Saturday.

My one year turned into two years because they changed elders over the Preparatory Class. Then it was finally time to preach my initial sermon. Bishop Morton would finally be able to call me one of his ministers. I preached at the same location that God had showed me in a dream. I was at the uptown location (*the church was known as one church in two locations)* and I was so glad, see, the east location was the largest location, and I didn't want to do my initial sermon there. I preached, "Turn the Switch On." It was okay, I didn't think I did well but everyone else felt differently. Now I was Minister Brenda A. Burton! WOW a preacher! I wanted to continue to work with Feed the Hungry Ministry because I loved it so much.

I was in charge of the preaching program. Whenever the preacher didn't show, I was allowed to preach. I was glad when they didn't show because I always had a Word to tell the people. When I did the invitation to Christ, a lot of people would come up to get saved. Later on, I started helping out the Mission Society Ministry that gave out baskets during Thanksgiving. I enjoyed giving out the baskets each year. It felt so good knowing that I played a part in helping someone.

One year, we had more baskets than we needed, so I told them to give the extra baskets to me. My car was loaded up with ten baskets, and I rode around town and gave them to whomever God led me to give them to. I was able to bless ten families with some food. I will never forget that God told me to stop by the St. Bernard's Project. I was at a building in the projects (This area was known for robbing and killing folks). God told me to stop at this particular section of the building, I had the basket in my hand walking down the sidewalk up to the doors. There were people sitting on the steps talking. They started to clear the steps so that I could pass by them. They said to me, "We *are sorry for blocking your way.*" You are not blocking my way," I replied. Immediately God told me to give the basket to one of the ladies that was sitting on the steps. After I gave her the basket, she began to cry. The other lady began to scream, "*I told you that God would do it!!*"

The lady began to explain to me that her friend had just told her that she didn't have any food to eat and she had no idea what she would feed her children on tomorrow. She knew that God sent me. Again, I was glad I listened to the voice of the Lord.

My life with the Ministerial Alliance was going very well. In 1996 I was nominated (*during Ministerial Alliance Annual Day*) for "New Minister of the Year" and for Mission Work awards. Later that year I was issued my certificate of license. Now I really was a preacher. I had engagements all the time. I did many radio broadcasts, telling my testimony. I was also on World Harvest Program telling my testimony, and was soon elevated to another position in the Alliance.

Another minister and I were responsible for the 8:00 a.m. service at Greater St. Stephen Church. We had to make sure that there were ministers at each aisle. We had to make sure the scripture and prayer was assigned each Sunday because we had to be sure that there were ministers there to pray with the people once they came forward. We had to fill in if someone was not in his or her place. The next year, I received the Mission Work award again. I enjoyed being a preacher some days. Other days it was so hard. It seemed as if the devil himself would show up.

CHAPTER TEN

THE TEST

I titled this chapter "The Test" because God allowed the devil to test me to see if I would go back.

AFTER SERVICE ONE NIGHT, Sister Frankie* approached me. She told me that Co-Pastor Morton wanted to know if I would put my testimony in the WOE (Women of Excellent) Magazine. I gladly said yes, and we set a day to discuss the details. I began working on my article for the magazine. It wasn't easy to walk down that memory lane. I thought it was going to be easy writing down my past, but it wasn't. I had to pray day and night. I wanted to quit writing the article several times but I continued to write because God told me a lot of people would be blessed by the article.

While still writing the article, one day, Bruce*, a male friend of mine, walked up to me and started telling me that he loved me and wanted me to be his wife. I cared about him as a friend, but not as a boyfriend. Because he was very nice to my family and me, I eventually began having feelings for him as well and he was so happy.

I was on my way to pick him up for church one Sunday and the Lord began to speak to me, but I wasn't listening. When I arrived at his apartment, the Lord was still speaking, but I was still not listening. When I knocked on his door, he answered, but wasn't dressed. He had on a t- shirt and a pair of jeans. I angrily asked him, "*Why aren't you dressed?*" He just replied that he was on his way to take a shower. As he proceeded toward the shower, I asked him, "*Whose jacket is this on the chair?*" He yelled out the door, "*Oh' Brenda, I found it outside the door.*" I told him, "*Don't you know spirits travel on things.*" He just replied, "*Brenda, you are always so deep.*" The Lord started speaking again for a third time, but I still wasn't listening. As I was standing in his living room, I looked into his bedroom and saw his pants on the ironing board. I walked into his bedroom to help him out (to hurry him up). I started to iron his pants. I turned around to look into his closet for his shirt. I was looking for the one that went with his pants. Well, I will never forget what I found in the closet. It wasn't his shirt. It was a naked man lying on the floor of his closet. The first thing I saw when I looked in the closet was his feet. I screamed and ran into the bathroom yelling, "*It's a naked man in your closet.*" He pulled back the shower curtain, and said, "*I know.*" It never dawned on me what was going on. He walked out of the shower and said, "*Brenda, I am so sorry.*" I just looked at him with tears in my eyes. He said, "*We just finished making love. I am so sorry.*" The naked guy had gotten dressed and started walking toward us. He said, "*He is lying, we were not making love. You are making him say that.*" I turned around and told the naked guy, "*Shut up, devil. I am not talking to you. I am talking to him who is supposed to be saved.*" I turned and walked out of the door.

As I was driving back to church, the devil started saying, "*Men are no good, men are no good. Go back to women. They never did you like this.*" I told the devil, "*You are a liar, he might not be any good, but God has one for me.*" I made it back to the church. It was so hard for me to lift my hands up to God, and I just sat there with tears in my eyes. Then all of a sudden, this minister gave me a note. The note said "*Your deliverance is in your praise.*" I got up and started praising God for what He had done for me. God allowed me to be protected from the devil. I realized that God was constantly trying to stop me from being hurt, but I wasn't listening. From now on, I will listen to the voice of the Lord.

I was on my way to tell friends what had just happened to me. I ran into Bruce. He wanted to talk to me, but I did not feel like talking, I was too hurt. The Lord spoke to me and told me to talk to him, and I had to obey His voice. God told me to help him get his deliverance just like I got mine, "*It is not about a relationship with Bruce. I want you to help him, now.*" Bruce asked me out to eat and talk. I told him okay. He also told me that he needed my help to stay delivered from that lifestyle. He informed me that when he got upset with his father, that is when he felt like sinning. We had a long discussion, and he agreed to come to Free Indeed regularly.

CHAPTER ELEVEN

THE MOVE OF GOD

I titled this chapter "The Move Of God" because of God's movement in a service; many were delivered.

I FOUND OUT LATE THE SAME WEEK that I had to preach that Wednesday. God gave me a word to speak on the topic, "The Peace of God." I talked about how the peace of God had kept me throughout the past week. I also realized why the devil tried to make my testimony a lie. I had been working on the magazine, and the devil had been telling me that as soon as the article came out, I would be talked about at church and lose my job, as well when everyone found out about my testimony. I was a little afraid, and was planning on staying away from my church and my job. I decided to beat the devil at his own game. The week the article came out, I took it to work, showed it to my supervisors, and told them about my testimony.

I busted into church with my head held high. Everything went well and I was fine. I was asked to be the sales manager of WOE Magazine and happily accepted the offer. We went on our first trip to Atlanta Ga. I had a wonderful time. I got to stay at my stepbrother's home. When I returned from the trip, my daddy was sick and he found out he had cancer. We started talking on the phone every other day. Our relationship was growing closer, and I was spending more time with my daddy. I finally had what I wanted all of my life, to spend time with my daddy. I just loved every moment of it, too.

The next trip was Charlotte, North Carolina. They were going to let me fly, but I told them that I wouldn't mind driving and that way someone else could go with me. Minister Francine* volunteered to go with me. We left that Wednesday evening and took turns driving for 12 hours. We made it to North Carolina Thursday morning. When we finally got to the hotel, we just fell out on the bed. We were so tired, yet excited about being in North Carolina. We showered, changed, and got the directions to the church.

We attended the evening service. They showed us so much love. We set up the WOE Magazine table and sold a lot of magazines. We were treated like royalty, and we had a wonderful time that day. The next day was good also. There was a luncheon that was held in the same hotel where we were staying. The Lord told me not to eat. I didn't know why, but I just listened. I went to the room to lie down. When I made it back down, it was time for the program. It was truly a wonderful program. We had a few hours before service that night. We did not want to be late so we made it to the service early, set up the WOE Magazine table and went in to wait for the service to start. We were so eager to get there that we forgot the magazine with my testimony in it.

The church reminded me so much of Greater St. Stephen Church. Their Co-Pastor was the splitting image of Co-Pastor Morton. They had the same kind of car, they dressed alike, and her mannerisms were just like Co-Pastor Morton's. I couldn't believe it. They had another pastor hosting the service. She told us that she would introduce us in a few minutes. Minister Francine and I had already discussed who would go first, Minister Francine went first and she introduced me last. I got up and told the people of God about my testimony, how God had delivered me from homosexuality. The whole church just went crazy. They were so excited about my deliverance from the lifestyle. I had told my story before but never had I seen a reaction like that. They were truly happy for me. The hosting pastor told them that God was giving them another chance to be free then she called me up and told me that God wanted to really get the people free. She told the people to come down and I would minister to them.

A lot of people came down to be delivered, and I was asked to lay hands on all those people. As I laid hands on them, another pastor prayed for me as I prayed for them. I noticed as the other pastor prayed for me the anointing was flowing. *So I found out that while you are laying hands on someone, you need someone to be praying for you also.* The anointing was at a very high level. I had never seen the anointing at such a great magnitude. The hosting pastor was getting ready to introduce the speaker for that night. She made the statement, "Some more folks will be delivered before the night is over."

Right before the speaker came up, the Bishop of the church, came to the microphone to speak under the anointing of the Holy Ghost. The people were still laid out on the floor. The Bishop said, "**God said that I've been gracious enough unto you, to give you an opportunity to walk away from death, but you won't do it, so God said judgment be upon you. Every homosexual, I am going to expose you and my judgment is upon you, even those in high places. You don't want folks to know, but God said judgment is upon you because I have given you an opportunity, now. He is** giving you one more chance before His word comes forward. If you walk away from this opportunity, you are going to walk into judgment, and that judgment will be utter death. God said if you come now, He will give you life."

After the Bishop left the microphone, more people came down for deliverance. I was asked to come and minister to the other people, and the other pastor came right behind me and laid hands on me. I ministered to this young lady and a couple of young men, then I turned around and saw this little boy about 8 years old. I got really mad at the devil. I turned around again and there was a little girl about 7 years old. I was very angry to see these little babies being bound by this spirit. *See the devil doesn't care who he gets into homosexuality, you could be blind, crippled, and crazy. He just doesn't care he is trying to take everyone that he can. Please don't get caught up in that lifestyle. I have been there and I can tell you that is not where you belong. It is a trick of the enemy, he is lying to you. Woman you are beautiful, man you are handsome, what you are looking for you already have it. Just look on the inside of your heart, and please know the devil doesn't play fair.*

We had to take orders for the magazine with my testimony. We had a lot of names to take down because they really wanted to read the article, and they even paid in advance for the magazine. We got out of church about 1:30 a.m. in the morning. We had a wonderful time in the Lord. They raised over 10 thousand dollars that night, and I witnessed them give the money to another ministry. God is going to bless them mightily. We went out to eat, and I was very hungry, but I didn't eat hardly anything. I guess I was too busy thinking about that little girl and boy. Finally I got to bed. The next morning, we were running a little bit late for service because I was so tired. When we got to the service a lot of the Pastors asked me if I would be willing to come to their church and speak. I gladly said yes because I wanted to see people set free.

The last service went very well. Then we said our good-byes and headed for home. I hated to leave I felt a pull to stay, but we had to be back in Louisiana the next day. As we were riding back home, Francine and I talked about what had just taken place in the last two days. We had a glorious time in the Lord. I was looking out of the window saying goodbye to North Carolina. As we were approaching South Carolina, I felt in my spirit that I would be back there to stay. Of course I dismissed those feelings quickly, I couldn't possibly move to North Carolina. We made it back to Louisiana and told everyone about our trip. My pastor had heard about the move of God, and he was very proud of me.

CHAPTER TWELVE

THE TRANSITION

I titled this chapter "The Transition" because of God's plan to move me to Greensboro, North Carolina.

IN NOVEMBER 1998, the Women of Excellence was having a retreat at Del Lago Resort in Conroe, Texas. The forecast was calling for it to be flooding in Conroe due to a Hurricane hitting the area. Some people at the church were telling us to make sure we took a boat with us. Some people cancelled out of going because they were scared. But I still had my plans to go I rented a car and a minister and I got on the highway.

When we arrived at the resort the people told us that yesterday water was everywhere. There was no water in sight except for the beach and the pool. They told us "You all must be some praying women." I videoed the service with my equipment. The sound didn't come out to well because I used a new video camera. During the retreat, we did a lot of activities that drew us closer to the Lord.

I remember writing my prayer requests down and attaching it to a balloon. Seeing my prayer requests go up in that beautiful blue sky just made me feel like God was getting a special delivery from me. I remember some of my requests. I asked about spiritual things. I wanted God to give me a double anointing. I wanted God to take me to another level in Him. I was invited by another pastor during the retreat to come and minister at her church. I had a good time. I hated to leave the resort. Little did I know that another trip was just around the corner.

In December 1998, I was scheduled to go on another Retreat for the WOE (Women of Excellence) Magazine Staff sponsored by Co- Pastor Debra B. Morton. We rode on the big WOE bus. We were on our way to Destine, Florida to work on ideas for the magazine. The beaches were so white. I had never seen a beach that white before. We took turns cooking the meals for everyone. Co-Pastor Morton drove up in her car the very next day. It seemed like we had the whole resort to ourselves. I was enjoying what God was doing with me. I got up and went to the beach to talk to God. It felt so good to walk in the white sand and wade through the water and look at the blue sky. I was feeling so good that I really wanted to stay forever. Some of them went shopping (Women have to go shopping). A couple of us stayed at the resort and went to the health spa.

After I got back from Florida, my ticket to North Carolina was there. Now, I was off to Greensboro, North Carolina. I brought some of the magazines with my testimony in it. I attended the church and the power of God was present just like in Charlotte. People were delivered and set free. In the middle of me speaking, the Lord told me that I would be coming back there to stay. I immediately said "No Lord." I told God that he would have to speak very clear to me in order for me to move to Greensboro, NC. I stayed an extra day to see Bishop Morton. He was speaking at a local church in Greensboro. His armour bearer didn't recognize me because I had on make-up.

I kept on begging God not to send me to Greensboro. Then God reminded me of what I told him. I told God long ago "Send me, I'll go. God please speak very loud and clear before I move anywhere I do not want to make any mistakes." And He did, everywhere I went, people kept telling me that I was getting ready to move. Then one day I ran into one of my friend's friend. He told me that he was moving to North Carolina. Then I ran into that same friend again and he told me again that he was moving to Greensboro, North Carolina. I told him that he was being used by God to tell me something. He had no idea what I was talking about. Every time someone would come and speak at the church they would always say things like, "Listen to God, even if He asks you to leave your family." I kept hearing the word "Transition" and how I would be moving. I finally went to the store to purchase an atlas so that I would know where I was moving to.

I told my daddy, "The Lord is telling me to move to North Carolina." He just said, "You are not moving anywhere" and he just laughed. One day, January 1999, I went to see my daddy with my sister and brother-in-law. He told me that he was ready to go home and be with the Lord. I told him, "No! we have just started to spend time together. I don't want you to go." I went to see him with my friend the next day, hoping that he had changed his mind. He wasn't feeling well, and I didn't want to make him get upset.

Well, the next day I was going to see him, but he died and I was sad. I wanted more time with him. I called his house and they told me that the people had just left with his body. I rushed out of the house to see him one more time. I went to the mortuary and I begged the guy to let me see him one more time. They had just got there. They told me that they would let me see his body. They asked me if I could handle seeing his body. I told them "Yes of course." It hit me later. I shouldn't have asked to see his body. I was messed up. My sister came down to be with me and we went to see my step-mom. They asked my sister if she would sing on the program. They didn't ask me anything. I was a little upset. My sister Linda came from Florida and Lil Johnny and ToJohnnica came by the house. They were all in tears. My brother Torrance from Atlanta didn't make it to the funeral, due to an accident. He hit a deer or should I say the deer hit him.

The funeral started at 8:00 p.m. We got there at 8:00 p.m. on the dot. When we walked into the church, everyone was already seated. We did not have anywhere to sit. I was very mad. I did not think it was fair for my sisters, brother and me to be without a seat. Some people finally got up and gave us a seat. We were spread all over the church. Some sat in the front, the middle, the back. My daddy would not have been happy about that. My sister Joyce sang and I requested that I have a spot on the program. They couldn't refuse me in front of all those people. I told them "It is a shame that my siblings and I did not have a seat to sit down." I told them, "My daddy would be very disappointed about that." Then I went on to say, "I thank God for the time that my daddy and I had to together and nothing could take that away." My daddy was gone and I started thanking God for the days I had with him.

Later on that week, my aunt called me and told me that she was glad that I went with my daddy to his attorney to get his will done. I told my aunt that I had never gone to his attorney with him. She told me that the attorney had informed her that his daughter named Brenda had been present during the signing. I had no idea what she was talking about. My step mom pulled a fast one on us. I didn't do anything about it because I was still hurting. Later, I found out that she had to move out of her house because she kept seeing my daddy. I was missing my daddy but life had to go on. I started thinking about the last two years that my daddy and I spent together.

I focused more on my relationship with God. I had a lot of engagements to preach at different churches. Evangelist White* invited me to speak at her "100 Women in White" program. She asked me if I would bring women from Greater St. Stephen Church to do the whole program that night. I got permission from my Co-Pastor Morton and Ministerial Alliance's President to go ahead and I asked the women if they wanted to go. I had a lot of women eager to go. I divided the time that they had allotted me so that two women from my church would be able to speak. We took the church's van and several cars. Programs were made by my dear friend Frank*. He put my picture on the programs. I also had envelopes made for seed time offerings. We went down to my home town with a spirit of Excellence (Thanks to Bishop & Co-Pastor Morton).

I prayed for everyone. My mother still tells me of this one lady that I prayed for. She is still talking about how she was healed at that women's program. The next week, I was in invited to do a "100 Women in Red" program. I had to speak on the blood of Jesus. Some of my family members came and got saved I was so happy. Seemed like, I was speaking almost every week. God was still speaking about me moving to North Carolina. I really did not want to leave my family and be out there all alone. I was willing to do whatever God wanted me to do. I knew that I had told God that I would do whatever He wanted me to do. I just had to trust God with everything.

CHAPTER THIRTEEN

THE CONCEPTION OF THE BOOK

I titled this chapter "The Conception of the Book" because when I moved to North Carolina, God began the conception of this book.

MONTHS HAD PASSED BY, and later I was promoted to Vice President of the Ministerial Alliance. *Wow, God saw my faithfulness and promoted me.* I was excited and surprised about the elevation. Things were going very well and my duties had increased. I had to be at the church real early to make sure everything went well for service. (*To whom much is given much is required.*). I knew that my duties would increase, and I was eager to serve the people of God. Everything in my life was going very well. I did not want anything to change.

Miranda wasn't excited about moving. She had so many friends, and she really didn't want to leave them. I told her that she would meet new friends. She knew that I wasn't going to leave her in Louisiana. Ministerial Alliance gave me a surprise birthday party after one of our monthly meetings. I was really going to miss the alliance; they had been really good to me.

I will never forget August 1999, the annual day for Ministerial Alliance. We were planning a big celebration for annual day. We were planning on giving a lot of gifts to everyone. We were nominating many ministers for different awards. We were so excited about the upcoming program. We were planning to have a big celebration for the annual day. I was kind of sad, knowing that the day would be approaching real fast, and I would be moving away. I would really miss everyone. I hated to leave, but I knew I must listen to the voice of the Lord.

Annual Day came and excitement was in the air. I was in for a very big surprise. They nominated me for the 1999 Minister of the Year. I was surprised. They also nominated me for 1999 Special Recognition for Mission Work. They sure fooled me. I had no idea. I received two awards. They gave me another surprise, and that was a going away party. I thought we were planning a gathering with all the ministers and elders, but it was a party for me, and my daughter videoed everything. All the ministers and the elders came up to me and gave me encouraging words. Some of them even planted over $600 dollars into my pocket. I just cried the whole night. When it was my time to say something, I couldn't get past the tears. I received so many hugs and gifts that I just thanked God. *God had only told me to pack my stuff and He would take care of everything else. So I wasn't worried about the money. I knew God would make a way somehow. I said my goodbyes and some of the people who were helping me pack and move asked me what time I was leaving. (I had no idea because I was waiting on God to move). I didn't have any money to rent the U-haul. I knew that I needed $1,000 dollars for the U-haul. I wasn't even counting the money for gas and food.*

A pastor from Greensboro, North Carolina was in town and she asked me, "Do you have all the money you need for the U-haul?" I told her I was lacking $350 dollars from the $1000 dollars that I needed. She gave me the remaining balance that I needed for the U-haul. I dropped her off at her appointment. I still wasn't thinking about the gas money for the U-haul. One of the sisters from the church came to help me finish the last little packing. She asked me to call another rental place because I might be able to find something cheaper. Well we did; we found another truck the same size for only $557 dollars. That meant that we had money for gas and food. God is so good. The Ministers and Elders had already gotten me over half the way. God didn't tell me anything about getting the money for moving He only told me to pack and not worry. I picked up the Pastor from her appointment and I told her the good news about the truck. She offered to help me go and pick up the truck. She drove my car while I drove the U-haul back to my apartment. I dropped her off at the airport, and I told her that we would see her in about 48 hours.

Back at the apartment we started to load the items on to the truck. It didn't take that long to load everything on to the truck. We spent one more night in the apartment.

I woke up the next morning early ready to get on the highway. Elder Small* had volunteered to drive me all the way to North Carolina. The pastor was willing to fly him back home. I would miss that apartment. I had been there since I was saved. I had so much help that I really didn't have to pick up anything. God is so good, and He is always on time. He is just so awesome and right on time. Before we got on the interstate, we made one more stop at the corporate headquarters of Greater St. Stephen. I had to take care of some last minute business for Ministerial Alliance.

We got on the road headed for Greensboro, North Carolina. I drove my car and Elder Small drove the U-haul. We didn't want to hook up the car to the U-haul because it was kind of hard to control. We left New Orleans, Louisiana about 5:00 p.m. and were headed to Greensboro. My heart was beating a little fast because I was anxious to get there. We took our time getting there. We followed each other. We took turns switching driving the U-haul and the car. Finally we were both tired of driving around 3:00 a.m. We pulled over to the rest area to get some sleep. I really couldn't sleep after being there for over 20 minutes. I was ready to try and start back driving. We got back on the interstate and we finally made it to Greensboro. Wow it took us 16 hours to make a 12 hour trip.

We made it to Greensboro, North Carolina. I was thanking God for the safety of the trips. He kept us from all hurt and harm on that dangerous highway. Miranda kind of slept all the way there until we stopped to eat. She woke up. A pastor met us as soon as we got off the interstate. We followed her to the apartment. She paid the rent and the deposit of the apartment. I had light, cable and telephone in my name. Everything was paid for when I moved in the apartment. My rent and bills were paid for at least four months. My daughter and I never missed a meal. I was finally in Gods perfect place at His perfect time.

If I had never obeyed God's voice to move to Greensboro, North Carolina, you would not be reading this book right now. It took four years to deliver this baby. The labor pains were excruciating and finally it's over. Thank you Jesus!

CHAPTER FOURTEEN

THE TRANSFORMATION

I titled this chapter "The Transformation" because it tells about how God transformed my life little by little.

MY TRANSFORMATION BEGAN IN 1993, when I received the Lord Jesus Christ as my Lord and Savior. This was the beginning of my process of transformation. The Lord transformed me into the woman of God He had ordained me to be. In 1994, I purchased my first purse. I never recalled carrying a purse. After I purchased the purse, I was confused as to what to put in it. I had no clue of what even belonged in a purse! I started stuffing everything into the purse. I was wondering how I got all that stuff into my back pocket. I was used to carrying a man's wallet. Now, I was carrying a purse for the first time in my life. I was a little nervous about carrying it because the devil kept saying, "You look like a man carrying a purse."

There was always a battle going on in my mind. The devil kept saying things to me every time I would purchase something that represented a woman. He would say things like *"You are a man trapped inside a woman's body"*, *"You look like a fool trying to be a woman"*, which is a lie from the pit of Hell. Please my brothers and sisters don't be fooled by the enemy. He will lie to you because he is the father of lies. Don't listen to him. You are who God made you, a mighty man of God, and a mighty woman of God. I told the devil that

I am T. S. O. C., Totally Sold Out for Christ. I told him that I am who God say I am.

All of my attire was men clothing. I would shop at all of men's stores, I would buy my ties and suspenders to match my shirts. God took me from dressing like a man to dressing like a woman. I gave all of my clothes to my brother and my nephews, and God provided me clothing. People gave me clothing, eventually my closet was full of women's clothing.

The next thing was my first pair of earrings. I bought the baby studs. They were the only ones in which I was comfortable. I went from the studs to real tiny baby earrings. I later graduated to the next size. They were still very small, but they were bigger than the ones before. Finally I moved to the regular sized ones. Please, my sisters and my brothers, don't try to go ahead of God. Many people wanted me to listen to them, but I had to go through my process of transformation according to God's guidelines. Now I am wearing the big earrings and I feel very comfortable. It was a process and God did it.

The next transformation that happened in my life was when God lead me to take some Glamour Shot pictures. When the lady finished making me over, I did not know who I was. I was so beautiful that I could not believe it was me. See the devil did not want me to see the woman inside of me. I never thought that I could look like that. I just said WOW! I am so sorry that I did not get a chance to purchase those pictures.

The next transformation was when I cut my curl into a bob hair style. The cut really made me look more feminine. My friend Leonard videoed the cut because he said it was history being made. I received a lot of compliments about the cut. I was so glad that I finally did it.

Before I made the move to Greensboro, North Carolina, the Lord told me to do one more thing. And that was for me to take the curl out of my hair. It was time for me to get a perm. I battled with that one for awhile. Then I finally did it. Another brick was being put into history. The curl was so easy to manage and a perm had to be worked with all the time. But I obeyed the voice of the Lord. You must remember that I never remember dressing like a woman. I never did girly stuff, so all this was so new to me.

God is still transforming me, even as I write this book. This transformation is a life long transformation. It is still an on-going process. Just the other day, the Lord told me it was time to add color to my hair. It looks wonderful and I am so happy that I did it.

Now you should understand why God had me to name this book *Transformation*. He continues to transform my life in Him. Romans 12:2 tells us "And be not conformed to this world: but be ye transformed by the renewing of your mind, that ye may prove what is that good, and acceptable, and perfect, will of God." Continue to let God transform you and not man. Everything will happen at God's perfect timing.

May this book help you to become free from whatever weight and sin which so easily besets you. God bless you and I love you.

Thanks goes out to my daughter Miranda, who told me to add this chapter to the book.

~Minister Brenda A. Burton

ABOUT THE AUTHOR

B RENDA A. BURTON is from the Cajun state Louisiana. She lived all of her life in Louisiana until God called her to North Carolina. She is the mother of one lovely daughter named Miranda who is currently attending college. When she was 12 years old, God told her that she would do something to impact the world. She knew that she would not become the President of the United States, but that she would write a book or something. She has a Bachelor of Social Work degree, and over 10 years of experience working with people with disabilities.

She was called into ministry in 1994 and preached her first sermon in May 1996. She received her official license in October 1996 and received a plaque for "New Minister of the Year." Also, in 1996 she was named "Woman of the Year" for "Free Indeed." In 1999 she received two awards, "Minister of the Year' and "Special Recognition for Mission Work'. She has been on numerous radio and television shows telling her testimony.

Proverbs 11:30b states "He that winneth souls is wise. Her number one goal in life is to win a lot of souls to Christ. To win the lost at any cost is what she is willing to do. She admonishes saints not to clean the fish before they catch them. She tells this short story:

One day I was out witnessing in the projects with the Evangelism Ministry. This guy came up and everyone thought that he was a girl, but I knew he was a man. Anyway,

I talked to him and invited him to church. He said that he couldn't come that day, but he would come one day. Well, one day I ran into him again. He was at my apartment complex visiting a friend. I asked him to come and go with me to church. He said, "Yes, I will go with you." Mind you, he had on a halter top and some shorts that were short and some heels that were very tall. I did not ask him to change clothes. I began to pray for the people at church. It was deliverance service night. I prayed that they would not look at him, but pray for him.

When we got the church, they were selling t-shirts. I bought my daughter and myself one. I looked at him, and I asked him if he wanted one. He said yes. Now when he put the shirt on, it looked as if he had on a dress. I could tell that he was really uncomfortable in church, so I leaned over and asked him if he wanted me to try and find him some pants. He said, "Yes, please." I called Tony and he brought a pair of his pants to church. The guy put the pants on, and that is how the Lord changed his attire in the church. We dressed him in the church. I didn't try to clean him before he was caught. He got saved that night when Bishop Morton made the altar call. Glory be to God!

COMMENTS FROM PASTORS

Minister Burton you have been faithful in your deliverance. I have seen you trusting in the word of God. You obey the move of God when you left for North Carolina. I think God had enriched you with a lot of things of Him and His ways. You are going to be successful in His work. I am delighted to see the book come to pass. Wish you great success.

Brother In-Law
Pastor Anthony Cox
Westside COGIC
184 Murray Rd
Ponchatoula, LA. 70454

To Minister Brenda Burton

What a blessings that the Lord God has for you! Eyes have not seen; nor ear has heard the things that God has for you because you love Him! Praise Him! Praise Him! May this book be an inspiration to all that are in the bondage to sin. God bless you and I love you.

Abner L. Fortson
Senior Pastor – Christ of Calvary Church
500 S. 61st Street
Philadelphia, PA. 19143

"If the Son therefore shall make you free, Ye shall be free Indeed," John 8:36

The Body of Christ must come to realize that there is nothing too hard for God. God is the God that specializes in the impossible. Most people believe that men and women who have lived homosexual lifestyles cannot be changed. I wholeheartedly disagree. God is still setting the captives free and performing miraculous feasts of deliverance in the lives of many of these same people who were considered outcasts because of their past sins. For Christians to say that God can't deliver homosexuals and lesbians is to deny and limit the very power of the Almighty God. The Bible clearly states in 2 Corinthians 5:17 that "If any man be in Christ, he is a new creature, old things are passed away and behold all things are become new." That includes new men and new women, regardless of their past. Like all others, people must be given time to develop in their Christian character and demeanor. Deliverance is instantaneous, but sanctification is a process.

The Christian church must learn to embrace persons who have renounced their former lifestyles and provide support for them to live godly and sanctified lives. If the church does not learn to accept these former prisoners of sexual perversion, they will soon return to places where they felt loved and accepted, namely bars and communities which promote their former proclivities. I wish to personally commend

Minister Brenda A. Burton for her tremendous stand for holiness and her ministry to women across the world. I have witnessed the transforming of her life from being rough and masculine to a beautiful, feminine young lady. This could only have happened as the Lord transformed her from the inside out by the power of the Holy Spirit. As we have both been delivered from this lifestyle and have ministered to countless men and women together, I am elated to know that

God is continuing to expand this ministry within the black community. African Americans are known for their ability to live in denial and secrecy. With this in mind, many homosexual strugglers have had to live secret lives of despair, danger, and shame. Most of these strugglers would leap at the opportunity to seek help if they knew they would be embraced and not disgraced. It's time to become modern-day healers for all people who seek to be free through the power of Jesus Christ. Will you be a vessel of healing or a vessel of condemnation and ridicule? The choice is yours. Nevertheless, be aware that as a watchman for the Lord, the blood of all who are turned away will be required at your hand on that great and powerful Day of Judgment.

It is my prayer that the contemporary African American church becomes a place of healing and restoration. Thanks to the work of Minister Brenda Burton and others, I know that my prayer will be answered one day. Men and women will find a place of embracing refuge and Jesus will be ultimately glorified. Keep up the great work Minister Burton! You're a jewel in the Body of Christ.

Pastor Leon Senegar,
Senior Pastor
Original Morning Star Full Gospel Baptist Church
New Orleans, Louisiana

My lovely daughter, Miranda, of whom I am very proud.

Order Form

To order additional copies, fill out this form and send it along with your check, cash, or money order to: Brenda A Burton, P.O. Box 1615 Jacksonville, NC 28541
Cost per copy $10.00 plus $4.00 P&H.

Ship _____ copies of *Transformation* to:

Name_____

Address:_____

City/State/Zip:_____

__ Check box for signed copy

Please tell us how you found out about this book.
__ Friend   __ Internet
__ Book Store   __ Radio
__ Newspaper   __ Magazine
__ Other _____